The Twelfth Name on New Jerusalem's Wall Foundation

The Twelfth Name on New Jerusalem's Wall Foundation

Michael Copple

Copyright © 2025 by Michael Copple

All rights reserved. No part of this book may be reproduced in any manner whatsoever without written permission except in the case of brief quotations embodied in critical articles and reviews.

This book is a work of non-fiction.

Because of the dynamic nature of the Internet, any web addresses or links contained in this book may have changed since publication and may no longer be valid.

Scripture quotations are from the New King James Version unless otherwise noted as (NIV) New International Version, and (KJV) King James Version of the Bible.

Cover Design: Elfriede Copple
Editing and Interior Book Layout/ Design: Elfriede Copple

ISBN 978-1-7389735-7-6 (Paperback)
ISBN 978-1-7389735-8-3 (eBook)

First Printing, November 2025

CONTENTS

1. Who, What, When, Where, Why, and How? — 1
2. Who is the Lamb? — 2
3. Who Chose the Twelve Disciples? — 3
4. Why Judas Iscariot? For What Purpose? — 5
5. Who? / When? / Why? / Where? / What? — 8
6. Parenthesis: — 15
7. Stephen and Saul — 17
8. Why Would the Lord Jesus Consider Paul? — 20
9. Paul Suffered for the Savior's Name Sake — 24
10. Dignitaries Confronted the Apostles — 27
11. Paul Preached the Gospel — 29

12 | Where and What? 31

13 | When and How? 33

14 | Why Consider Paul? 36

15 | How Can We Know? 39

A NOTE TO THE READER 44
OTHER BOOKS BY MICHAEL 45
ABOUT THE AUTHOR 46

1

Who, What, When, Where, Why, and How?

In some situations, these questions need to be asked in order to gain full understanding of reasons and results.

The prophesied new city of Jerusalem will be surrounded with a *great and high wall* (Revelation 21:10-12). Disagreement as to whose names will be on the twelve wall foundations will be settled when we all get there to see for ourselves. But present controversy is spiritually unhealthy in the Church. Therefore, letting the Spirit lead the way to take a closer look into Scripture will hopefully quell the differences.

The prophecy tells us this:

> *The wall of the city had twelve foundations, and on them were the names of the twelve apostles of the Lamb.* Revelation 21:14 (NIV)

2

Who is the Lamb?

Who is the Lamb? Being obedient to His Father, the Lord Jesus Christ offered Himself as the sacrifice without blemish to die once for all. He died in place of the multitude of lambs that died before the Father sent Him.

When The Passover was instituted for Israel to be liberated from slavery in Egypt (and, today our freedom from bondage to sin), a lamb was killed as an offering, or sacrifice for sin:

> **Exodus 12:5** Your lamb shall be without blemish, a male of the first year; ye shall take *it* out from the sheep, or from the goats. (KJV)
>
> **John 1:29** The next day John seeth Jesus coming unto him, and saith, Behold the Lamb of God, which taketh away the sin of the world. (KJV)

Of course, the *Lamb* in Revelation 21:14 refers to the Son of God, the Lord Jesus Christ.

> **Revelation 21:14** The wall of the city had twelve foundations, and on them were the names of the twelve apostles of the Lamb. (NIV)

3

Who Chose the Twelve Disciples?

Who chose the twelve disciples, eleven of whom would become the Twelve Apostles?

No question about it, the Lord Jesus Himself selected each and every one. God the Father gave them to His Son Jesus, who tells us this:

John 17:12 "While I was with them in the world, I kept them in Your name. Those whom You gave Me I have kept; and none of them is lost except the son of perdition, that the Scripture might be fulfilled."

We see from His choices of the first twelve disciples the following names:

Matthew 4:18-22 [18]And Jesus, walking by the Sea of Galilee, saw two brothers, Simon called Peter [also called Cephas in John 1:42], and Andrew his brother, casting a net into the sea; for they were fishermen. [19]Then He said to them, "Follow Me, and I will make you fishers of men." [20]They immediately left *their* nets and followed Him. ²¹Going on from there, He saw two other brothers, James the son of Zebedee, and John his brother, in the boat with Zebedee their father, mending their nets. He called them, ²²and immediately they left the boat and their father, and followed Him.

Matthew 10:2-8 ²Now the names of the twelve apostles are these: first, Simon, who is called Peter, and Andrew his brother; James the son of Zebedee, and John his brother; ³Philip and Bartholomew [also called Nathanael in John 1:45]; Thomas [also called the Twin in John 11:16; 20:24; 21:2; and called Didymus in some Bible versions]; and Matthew the tax collector [also called Levi, the son of Alphaeus in Mark 2:14]; James, [also the son of Alphaeus in Mark 3:18], and Lebbaeus, whose surname was Thaddaeus [also called Judas the son of James in Luke 6:16]; ⁴Simon the Cananite [also called the Zealot in Luke 6:16], and Judas Iscariot, who also betrayed Him. ⁵These twelve Jesus sent out and commanded them, saying, "Do not go into the way of the Gentiles, and do not enter a city of the Samaritans. ⁸Heal the sick, cleanse the lepers, raise the dead, cast out demons. Freely you have received, freely give."

The original twelve are also named in the other three Gospels: Mark 3:16-19; Luke 6:14-16; and John 1:35-51, 6:5-8, 11:16, 20:24, 21:2

4

Why Judas Iscariot? For What Purpose?

If *the son of perdition* is he who would betray the Son of God, what was the purpose for choosing Judas Iscariot to be one of the twelve disciples? The Lord knew well that He would choose a new twelfth man to replace Judas Iscariot.

Of course, the reason was to fulfill prophecy. The Lord Jesus already knew Judas Iscariot would betray Him; The Holy Spirit, circa 850 BC, inspired David to prophesy the following:

> **Psalm 41:9** Even my close friend, whom I trusted, he who shared my bread, has lifted up his heel against me. (NIV)
>
> **Psalm 109:8** Let his days be few; and let another take his office. (KJV)

Furthermore, the Lord Jesus prophesied to the twelve when gathered at the table:

> **John 13:21b** "Most assuredly, I say to you, one of you will betray Me."

John 13:26 Jesus answered, "It is he to whom I shall give a piece of bread when I have dipped it." And having dipped the bread, He gave *it* to Judas Iscariot, *the son* of Simon.

Judas Iscariot indeed betrayed the Lord Jesus:

John 18:3-5 ³Then Judas, having received a detachment of *troops*, and officers from the chief priests and Pharisees, came there with lanterns, torches, and weapons. ⁴Jesus therefore, knowing all things that would come upon Him, went forward and said, "Whom are you seeking?" ⁵They answered Him, "Jesus of Nazareth." Jesus said to them, "I am He" And Judas who betrayed Him, also stood with them.

Why would the Savior choose such a one as Judas Iscariot? The Lord Jesus, who is Almighty, Sovereign God along with His Father, knew the character of Judas, the one who would betray Him. He also knew the quality, mindset, capabilities and learning aptitudes of the other eleven whom He chose.

Our God and Savior, the Lord Jesus Christ, knows our thoughts, our minds, and our hearts:

1 Samuel 16:7 But the LORD said to Samuel, "Do not look at his appearance or at his physical stature, because I have refused him. For *the LORD does* not *see* as man sees; for man looks at the outward appearance, but the LORD looks at the heart."

Psalm 94:11a The LORD knows the thoughts of man;... (NIV)

Matthew 9:4 But Jesus, knowing their thoughts, said, "Why do you think evil in your hearts?"

Matthew 12:25a And Jesus knew their thoughts,... (KJV)

Acts 15:8 God, who knows the heart, showed that he accepted them by giving the Holy Spirit to them, just as he did to us. (NIV)

5

Who? / When? / Why? / Where? / What?

Who?
In reading and discerning the Scriptures, the importance of recognizing punctuation marks and knowing who is speaking, and to whom is being spoken to, cannot be overemphasized. Take notice that to whom the risen Savior is speaking are the chosen eleven:

Mark 16:14-18 ¹⁴Later He appeared to the eleven as they sat at the table; and He rebuked their unbelief and hardness of heart, because they did not believe those who had seen Him after He had risen. ¹⁵And He said to them, "Go into all the world and preach the gospel to every creature. ¹⁶He who believes and is baptized will be saved; but he who does not believe will be condemned. ¹⁷And these signs will follow those who believe: In My name they will cast out demons; they will speak with new tongues; ¹⁸they will take up serpents; and if they drink anything deadly, it will by no means hurt them; they will lay hands on the sick, and they will recover."

When?

After the Lord's ascension the eleven disciples returned from the Mount of Olivet to Jerusalem.

Acts 1:12-17 ¹²Then they returned to Jerusalem from the mount called Olivet, which is near Jerusalem, a Sabbath day's journey. ¹³And when they had entered, they went up into the upper room where they were staying: Peter, James, John and Andrew; Philip and Thomas; Bartholomew and Matthew; James *the son* of Alphaeus and Simon the Zealot; and Judas *the son* of James. ¹⁴These all continued with one accord in prayer and supplication, with the women and Mary the mother of Jesus, and with His brothers, ¹⁵And in those days Peter stood up in the midst of the disciples (altogether the number of names was about a hundred and twenty), and said, ¹⁶"Men and brethren, this Scripture had to be fulfilled, which the Holy Spirit spoke before by the mouth of David concerning Judas, who became a guide to those who arrested Jesus; ¹⁷for he was numbered with us and obtained a part in this ministry."

Who does Scripture quote above in Acts 1:16-17? God's pure truth tells us it was Peter who *stood up, and said*...

It needs to be taken into account that Peter was speaking prior to him and the other disciples receiving the Holy Spirit.

Acts 1:4-5 ⁴And being assembled together with *them*, He commanded them not to depart from Jerusalem, but to wait for the Promise of the Father, "which," He said, "you have heard from Me; ⁵for John truly baptized with water, but you shall be baptized with the Holy Spirit not many days from now."

Recall, Peter had a reputation of making spur of the moment, snap decisions, reacting before thinking things out. For example, cutting off the ear of the high priest's servant (John 18:10); denying three times that he was one of the Lord's disciples (John 18:17, 25-27); requiring three attempts to answer the Lord Jesus when asked if he loved Him (John 21:15-17). It is likely that Peter, at this juncture, had *tasted* the Spirit (John 20:22; Heb. 6:5) but had not yet fully *absorbed* the Holy Spirit. Moreover, since God brought about the prophecy:

Psalm 109:8 Let his days be few; and let another take his office. (KJV)

Since God's Word prophesied the event, it seems most likely that God Himself would already know who would *take* Judas Iscariot's *office*. The Lord Jesus is quoted speaking of the need for the prophecy to be fulfilled:

John 17:12b "and none of them is lost except the son of perdition, that the Scripture might be fulfilled."

It is doubtful that the Father and Son needed any human intervention. Peter continues speaking:

WHO? / WHEN? / WHY? / WHERE? / WHAT? – | 11 |

Acts 1:20-21 ²⁰"For it is written in the Book of Psalms: '*Let his dwelling place be desolate, and let no one live in it*'; and '*Let another take his office.*' ²¹"Therefore, of these men who have accompanied us all the time that the Lord Jesus went in and out among us,"

Peter mistakenly said in verse 21, that *other men accompanied us all the time that the Lord Jesus went in and out among us*. John chapters 13 to 17 describe the Lord Jesus, being alone with His eleven chosen disciples in the Upper Room Discourse; clearly alone with them in His intercessory prayer in John 17; and again, alone with them the night of His capture in the Garden of Gethsemane where He told the captors:

John 18:8b-9 ⁸ᵇ"Therefore, if you seek Me, let these [the eleven] go their way," ⁹That the saying might be fulfilled which He spoke, "Of those whom You gave me I have lost none."

Continuing with Peter addressing the group:

Acts 1:22-26 ²²"beginning from the baptism of John to that day when He was taken up from us, one of these must become a witness with us of His resurrection." ²³And they proposed two: Joseph called Barsabas, who was surnamed Justus, and Mathias. ²⁴And they prayed and said, "You, O Lord, who know the hearts of all, show which of these two You have chosen [Take note that they comprehended that the Lord knows the hearts.] ²⁵to take part in this ministry and apostleship from which Judas by transgression fell, that he might go to his own place." ²⁶And they cast their lots, and the lot fell on Mathias. And he was numbered with the eleven apostles.

Was it the Lord's will to answer the disciples' prayer? We should ask, "Did God answer that prayer by agreeing with *their* choices?" Peter and the other ten disciples, in Acts 1:24 admitted that God does *know the hearts of all*, but they did not remember God saying that His thoughts and ways are not the same as ours. Do we know God's mind?

> **Isaiah 55:8-9** ⁸"For my thoughts are not your thoughts, neither are your ways my ways," declares the LORD. ⁹"As the heavens are higher than the earth, so are my ways higher than your ways and my thoughts than your thoughts." (NIV)

Acts 1:23 and 26 are the only two times and the last we hear of Mathias in God's Word. However, Mathias could possibly have acted as an apostle, either permanently, if God so approved, *or* he could have served until God might have replaced him after Paul was converted in AD 37. Then Paul spent three more years away (Galatians 1:17-18), and returned to Jerusalem in AD 40. We point this out because Paul was not yet considered to be *one of the twelve* who had seen the Lord Jesus during the 40 days (Acts 1:3) following the resurrection in AD 33. Mathias might have been considered to be one of the *twelve*:

> **1 Corinthians 15:7** After that He was seen by James, then by all the apostles.

Only our Sovereign God knows whether or not He answered the disciples' earlier prayer to consent to the lots they had cast. The Lord's answer to prayer is sometimes "Yes", sometimes "No", and other times "Wait". *If* He had assented to their prayer, then Mathias would be included with the term *all the apostles*. Only God knows the answer.

To avoid confusion, 1 Corinthians 15 verse 5 needs to be clarified. The verse having to do with Mathias is 15:7 above. It is the relevant verse having to do with Mathias. Here in verse 5, the term *the twelve*, refers to the 11 chosen *disciples*. (John 20:24) Not ordained yet as apostles, they are recorded in John 20:19-29 to have seen the Lord Jesus in that closed-door room:

> **1 Corinthians 15:5** and that He was seen by Cephas, then by the twelve.

It is noteworthy that the Day of Pentecost had not yet come, and the Holy Spirit had not yet indwelt the disciples nor the others gathered in that house—not until the next chapter's first two verses. When they prayed for God to show them which one He had chosen, they had not yet received the Holy Spirit:

> **Matthew 3:11** "I [John the Baptizer] indeed baptize you with water unto repentance, but He who is coming after me is mightier than I, whose sandals I am not worthy to carry. He will baptize you with the Holy Spirit." (Repeated in Mark 1:8; Luke 3:16; John 1:33)

When?

When was the Holy Spirit poured out? Fifty days after the Lord Jesus was resurrected, after having been dead for three days, the day of Pentecost was upon the disciples:

> **Acts 2:1-2** When the Day of Pentecost had fully come, they were all with one accord in one place. ²And suddenly there came a sound from heaven, as of a rushing mighty wind, and it filled the whole house where they were sitting. [Then and there they had absorbed the Holy Spirit!]

6

Parenthesis:

Example of Absorbing the Holy Spirit.

Upon trusting God's truth, repenting and believing the fact that Jesus shed His blood to forgive us of our sins, and died and was raised back to life three days later; we then, with the baptizing power of the Lord Jesus Christ, absorb the Holy Spirit. In other words, the Holy Spirit, even onto an assembled body of believers, comes from the Lord Jesus Christ:

Acts 19:1-6 While Apollos was at Corinth, Paul took the road through the interior and arrived at Ephesus. There he found some disciples [2]and asked them, "Did you receive the Holy Spirit when you believed?" They answered, "No, we have not even heard that there is a Holy Spirit." [3]So Paul asked, "Then what baptism did you receive?" "John's baptism," they replied. [4]Paul said, "John baptism was a baptism of repentance. He told the people to believe in the one coming after him, that is, in Jesus." [5]On hearing this, they were baptized into the name of the Lord Jesus. [6]When Paul placed his hands on them, the Holy Spirit came on them, and they spoke in tongues [languages] and prophesied [preached the Gospel Message]. (NIV)

Verse 6 calls for an explanation: in the earliest days of the Church Age, there were four times in the Book of Acts when the Holy Spirit was received:

1. In Act 2:2-4, the Day of Pentecost,
2. In Acts 8:16-17, when Peter and John laid hands on the Samaritans,
3. In Acts 10:44, at the home of Cornelius, *while Peter was still speaking these words* [The Gospel Message], *the Holy Spirit fell upon all those who heard the word*.
4. In regards to Acts 19:6, William MacDonald points out: "By giving *the Holy Spirit* through the laying on of Paul's *hands*, the Lord forestalled the possibility of a charge being made later that Paul was inferior to Peter, John, or the other apostles."

Today, with the completion of the Scriptures, MacDonald explains:
"The moment a person believes on the Lord Jesus Christ, he is indwelt by the Holy Spirit, he is sealed by the Holy Spirit; he receives the earnest of the Spirit; he receives the anointing of the Spirit; and he is baptized by the Spirit into the Body of Christ."

(End of the parenthesis.)

7

Stephen and Saul

When was Stephen stoned to death? About two years after the Church began at Pentecost:

Acts 7:59-60 ⁵⁹And they [Jewish elders & scribes] stoned Stephen as he was calling on God and saying, "Lord Jesus, receive my spirit." ⁶⁰Then he knelt down and cried out with a loud voice, "Lord, do not charge them with this sin." And when he had said this, he fell asleep [he died].

Acts 8:1a Now Saul was consenting to his [Stephen's] death...

Acts 8:3 ³As for Saul, he made havoc of the church, entering every house, and dragging off men and women, committing *them* to prison.

Soon after Stephen's death Saul prepared to go to Damascus: (When introduced in Acts 8:1, Paul was called by his Jewish name: "Saul". He is not called Paul until Acts 13:9.)

Acts 9:1-5 Then Saul, still breathing threats and murder against the disciples of the Lord, went to the high priest ²and asked letters from him to the synagogue of Damascus, so that if he found any who were of the Way, whether men or women, he might bring them bound to Jerusalem. ³As he journeyed he came near Damascus, and suddenly a light shone around him from heaven. ⁴Then he fell to the ground, and heard a voice saying to him, "Saul, Saul, why are you persecuting Me?" ⁵And he [Saul] said, "Who are You, Lord?" Then the Lord said, "I am Jesus, whom you are persecuting. It is hard for you to kick against the goads."

Paul undoubtedly knew he was persecuting the followers of Jesus, but now he is face-to-face with the brightest Light he had ever seen: The Lord Jesus Christ Himself!

Kick against the goads equates to *attempting to row a boat upstream against a strong current*. It could possibly mean that Paul knew in his conscience that persecuting the Lord and His followers was definitely wrong; but he had been driven to do so by Jewish, unbelieving malefactors. Paul possibly knew in his heart that as he was on the road to Damascus to persecute Christians, common sense—his good judgment of right and wrong—was telling him he was mistaken. God knows our thoughts (Psalm 139:2; Matthew 9:4), and when the Holy Spirit comes upon us, we receive a new heart and a new spirit; we become "born again". Thus, whenever we head off toward the world's ways instead of God's ways, we quickly perceive our thoughts and actions are struggling, and we come back instantaneously to follow Jesus. In Paul's case here, this redemption happened to him as soon as he realized he was face to face with the resurrected Lord Jesus Christ.

Believers corporately were called the *Way* before being called *Christians* at Antioch, circa AD 42. Today Christians worldwide are each a member of the body of Christ, the universal Church, of which the Lord Jesus Christ is the Head.

> **Acts 9:6** So he [Saul], trembling and astonished, said, "Lord, what do You want me to do?" Then the Lord said to him, "Arise and go into the city, and you will be told what you must do."

8

Why Would the Lord Jesus Consider Paul?

So why would anyone think the Lord Jesus would consider him to be an apostle? Paul was a notorious persecutor of the early church. Paul, being honestly, deeply, genuinely, sincerely, exceedingly remorseful writes:

> **1 Timothy 1:15** [15]Here is a trustworthy saying that deserves full acceptance: Christ Jesus came into the world to save sinners of whom I am the worst. (NIV)
>
> **Romans 9:1-3** I tell the truth in Christ, I am not lying, my conscience also bearing me witness in the Holy Spirit, [2]that I have great sorrow and continual grief in my heart. [3]For I could wish that I myself were accursed from Christ for my brethren, my countrymen according to the flesh,

Why was Paul so deeply troubled? Why would anyone want to be sent to hell and the lake of fire in place of his Jewish brothers and sisters? And why were they being chastened by God?

Well, hadn't they continued believing they could be good enough to keep the Commandments—although they were not able and never did? And hadn't they advocated for the crucifixion of the very Son of God? And, have they done any better since? Don't they, to this day, still believe that being chosen above all other nations makes them *special* saints, the *apple of God's eye*? And don't they still believe in their good works and ritualistic services instead of believing in our God and Savior the Lord Jesus Christ?

Paul, in his flesh, being born a Jew, understood at least as well as any other Jew, that they and he had been utterly, *dead* wrong by not accepting Jesus as the Messiah.

Following his conversion, when he saw that the Lord Jesus had indeed been resurrected, his ways of conduct and thinking became a constant practice of righteousness. He wrote this explanation to the saints in Philippi:

> **Philippians 3:3** For we [believers: both Jews and Gentiles] are the circumcision [not physically, but spiritually, of the heart], who worship God in the Spirit, rejoice in Christ Jesus, and have no confidence in the flesh,

In other words, simply because Israelites were the chosen ones, it gives no assurance they will see the Promised Land. Philippians 3:3 calls for further explanation of four distinct phrases: W*e are the circumcision* means that our "old self" died with Christ on the cross (Romans 6:6). Believers are unable to serve God on their own merit; *God in the Spirit* of the Lord Jesus *fills us* and controls us. *Christ is all, and in all*

(Colossians 3:11). *Worship God in the Spirit* is real worship of the heart—not outward, not attention to self, not ritualistic methods, nor satisfying a selfish need to be noticed. "*True worshipers will worship the Father in spirit and truth*" (John 4:23). We *rejoice in Christ Jesus* means we glory in the Lord. We depend on Him totally. On our own we cannot be fruitful for Him. "*Without Me you can do nothing.*" (John 15:5b)

Back to Paul now. We *have no confidence in the flesh*; our sinful nature we received from Adam does not disappear. *For I know that in me (that is, in my flesh) nothing good dwells* (Romans 7:18)

> **Philippians 3:4-6** ⁴though I [Paul] also might have confidence in the flesh. If anyone else thinks he may have confidence in the flesh [for being undefiled Jewish], I more so: ⁵circumcised the eighth day, of the stock of Israel, *of* the tribe of Benjamin, a Hebrew of the Hebrews, concerning the law, a Pharisee; ⁶concerning <u>zeal</u>, <u>persecuting the church</u>, concerning the righteousness which is in the law, blameless. [Underlines are not Scripture; for emphasis only.]

Where Paul states he was "*a Hebrew of the Hebrews, concerning the law, a Pharisee*", it is quite possible he was also indicating that he was so extremely devoted that he was a Nazirite. Quoting from Smith's Bible Dictionary: "[A Nazirite is] one who was bound by a vow to be set apart from others for the service of God."

Acts 18:18b He [Paul] had *his* hair cut off at Cenchrea, for he had taken a vow.

(If Paul was indeed a Nazirite, he would have been forbidden to cut the hair of his head for life or until the period of his vow was fulfilled. We do not know the particulars of Paul's vow.) In the Old Testament, the parents made the vow before the birth of the Nazirite himself. It is plausible that Paul's parents put Paul into this sect; his father was a Pharisee:

Acts 23:6 But when Paul perceived that one part were Sadducees and the other Pharisees, he cried out in the council, "Men *and* brethren, I am a Pharisee, the son of a Pharisee, concerning the hope and resurrection of the dead I am being judged!"

Acts 9:15-16 [15]But the Lord said to him, [to Ananias] "Go, for he [Saul/Paul] is a chosen vessel of Mine to bear My name before Gentiles, kings, and the children of Israel [Jews]. [16]For I will show him how many things he must suffer for My name's sake."

Who bestowed Paul with such incredible abilities to perform miracles similar to what the Lord Jesus had done? Of course, the Savior Himself poured the Holy Spirit into Paul. We read much about the supernatural power demonstrated by Paul throughout the last half of the Book of Acts of the Apostles. We should take into account the first phrase of the Savior's last sentence that He spoke to the eleven prior to being taken up before their eyes:

Acts 1:8a "But you shall receive power when the Holy Spirit has come upon you"

9

Paul Suffered for the Savior's Name Sake

Examples of what Paul had to suffer for the Savior's Name Sake:

2 Corinthians 11:23-28 [23]Are they [other servants and apostles] ministers of Christ?—I *am* more: in labors more abundant, in stripes above measure, in prisons more frequently, in deaths often. [24]From the Jews five times I received forty *stripes* minus one. [25]Three times I was beaten with rods; once I was stoned; three times I was shipwrecked; a night and a day I have been in the deep; [26]*in* journeys often *in* perils of waters, *in* perils of robbers, *in* perils of the Gentiles, *in* perils in the city, *in* perils in the wilderness, *in* perils in the sea, *in* perils among false brethren; [27]in weariness and toil, in sleeplessness often, in hunger and thirst, in fastings often, in cold and nakedness—[28]besides the other things, what comes upon me daily; my deep concern for all the churches.

2 Timothy 3:10-12 [10]But you have carefully followed my doctrine, manner of life, purpose, faith, longsuffering, love, perseverance, [11]persecutions, afflictions, which happened to me at Antioch, at Iconium, at Lystra—what persecutions I endured. And out of *them* all the Lord delivered me. [12]Yes, and all who desire to live godly in Christ Jesus will suffer persecution.

Luke verified some of the events in Paul's perilous ministry:

Acts 13:49-51 [49]And the word of the Lord was being spread throughout all the region. [50]But the Jews stirred up the devout and prominent women and the chief men of the city, raised up persecution against Paul and Barnabas, and expelled them from the region. [51]But they shook off the dust from their feet against them, and came to Iconium. (See Matt. 10:14)

Acts 14:19 Then Jews from Antioch and Iconium came there; and having persuaded the multitudes, they stoned Paul *and* dragged *him* out of the city, supposing him to be dead.

Acts 16:20-24 [20]And they [the authorities of Philippi] brought them [Paul and Silas] to the magistrates, and said, "These men, being Jews, exceedingly trouble our city; [21]and they teach customs which are not lawful for us, being Romans, to receive or observe," [22]Then the multitude rose up together against them; and the magistrates tore off their clothes and commanded *them* to be beaten with rods. [23]And when they had laid many stripes on them, they threw *them* into prison, commanding the jailer to keep them securely. ²⁴Having received such a charge, he put them into the inner prison and fastened their feet in stocks.

10

Dignitaries Confronted the Apostles

Who were some of the dignitaries whom the Lord Jesus said the apostles would be *brought before—for* His *sake*?

The Lord Jesus gave to the eleven original disciples, the following directives:

Matthew 10:14 ¹⁴"And whoever will not receive you nor hear your words, when you depart from that house or city shake off the dust from your feet."

Matthew 10:16-20 ¹⁶"Behold, I send you out as sheep in the midst of wolves, therefore be wise as serpents and harmless as doves. ¹⁷But beware of men, for they will deliver you up to councils and scourge you in their synagogues. ¹⁸You will be brought before governors and kings for My sake, as a testimony to them and to the Gentiles. ¹⁹But when they deliver you up, do not worry about how or what you should speak. For it will be given to you in that hour what you should speak; ²⁰for

> it is not you who speak, but the Spirit of your Father who speaks in you."

Looking into Paul's historical journeys, the Lord's orders to the original disciples, it all seems to apply to Paul as well:

Paul spoke to both Festus—the Roman governor of Judea, and to King Agrippa—an Edomite (he was a Gentile)—also called Herod—6th Herod, or King of Judea.

Judea was a Roman imperial province. The Northern kingdom of Israel was exiled by the Assyrians in 722 BC, and the Southern Kingdom was overthrown by the Babylonian empire in 587 BC. Israel was not called Israel again until 1948. During the period in the early Church Age it was still called Judea, here's what Paul was saying to Festus the procurator [governor] and to King Agrippa of Judea:

> **Acts 26:24-29** [24]Now as he thus made his defense, Festus said with a loud voice, "Paul, you are beside yourself! Much learning is driving you mad!" [25]But he said, "I am not mad, most noble Festus, but speak the words of truth and reason. [26]For the king, before whom I also speak freely, knows these things; for I am convinced that none of these things escapes his attention, since this thing was done in a corner. [27]King Agrippa, do you believe the prophets? I know that you do believe." [28]Then Agrippa said to Paul, "You almost persuade me to become a Christian." [29]And Paul said, "I would to God that not only you, but also all who hear me today, might become both almost and altogether such as I am, except for these chains."

11

Paul Preached the Gospel

Paul not only *preached* the Gospel Message, but also *wrote* it in Epistles that have gone around the globe and are present today. For example:

1 Corinthians 15:1-2 Moreover, brethren, I declare to you first of all the gospel which I preached to you, which also you received and in which you stand, ²by which also you are saved, if you hold fast that word which I preached to you—unless you believed in vain. [some may have *tasted* the Spirit, but *spit it out* and did not *absorb* the indwelling Holy Spirit]

1 Corinthians 15:3-4 ³For I delivered to you first of all that which I also received: that Christ died for our sins according to the Scriptures, (Isaiah 53:12; Daniel 9:26) ⁴and that He was buried, and that He rose again the third day according to the Scriptures,

Paul was fulfilling and being obedient to the responsibilities of the Lord's command:

> **Mark 16:14-15** ¹⁴Later He appeared to the eleven as they sat at the table; and He rebuked their unbelief and hardness of heart, because they did not believe those who had seen Him after He had risen. ¹⁵And He said to them, "Go into all the world and preach the gospel to every creature."

12

Where and What?

Where was the ship wreck describing part of Paul's third journey in Acts 27?

It was near the Island of Malta in the Mediterranean Sea.

What happened and what was the ship carrying?

The ship was battered (*stern being broken by violence of the waves*), sinking with cargo and *two hundred and seventy-six persons*, including Paul.

What miraculous events took place on the island?

Acts 28:1 Once safely on shore, we found out that the island was called Malta. (NIV)

Acts 28:3-6 ³Paul gathered a pile of brush wood and, as he put it on the fire, a viper [serpent], driven out by the heat, fastened itself on his hand. ⁴When the islanders saw the snake hanging from his hand, they said to each other, "This man must be a murderer; for though he escaped from the sea, the goddess Justice has not allowed him to live." ⁵But Paul shook the snake off into the fire and suffered no ill effects [harm]. (Mark 16:18) ⁶The people expected him to swell up or sud-

|31|

denly fall dead; but after waiting a long time and seeing nothing unusual happen to him, they changed their minds and said he was a god. (NIV)

Acts 28:8-9 ⁸And it happened that the father of Publius lay sick of a fever and dysentery. Paul went in to him and prayed, and he laid his hands on him and healed him. ⁹So when this was done, the rest of those on the island who had diseases also came and were healed. (Mark 16:18)

13

When and How?

When was *Saul* known to be *Paul*?

Soon after the believers were first called *Christians* at Antioch in Northern Phoenicia near the Syrian border, Saul became known as Paul in Acts 13:9.

How could Paul have such power to cause a man to go blind?

Scripture below tells us how: He was filled with the Holy Spirit in the same way as the other eleven whom Jesus had chosen. The Lord Jesus said:

Acts 1:8 "But you shall receive power when the Holy Spirit has come upon you; and you shall be witnesses to Me in Jerusalem, and in all Judea and Samaria, and to the end of the earth."

Paul exerting his power:

Acts 13:8-12 ⁸But Elymas the sorcerer (for so his name is translated) withstood them, seeking to turn the proconsul [provincial governor] away from the faith. ⁹Then Saul, who also *is called* Paul, filled with the Holy

Spirit, looked intently at him ¹⁰and said, "O full of deceit and all fraud, *you* son of the devil, *you* enemy of all righteousness, will you not cease perverting the straight ways of the Lord? ¹¹And now, indeed, the hand of the Lord *is* upon you, and you shall be blind, not seeing the sun for a time," And immediately a dark mist fell on him, and he went around seeking someone to lead him by the hand. ¹²Then proconsul believed, when he saw what had been done, being astonished at the teaching of the Lord.

Acts 14:8-11 ⁸And in Lystra a certain man without strength in his feet was sitting, a cripple from his mother's womb, who had never walked. ⁹*This* man heard Paul speaking. Paul, observing him intently and seeing that he had faith to be healed, ¹⁰said with a loud voice, "Stand up on your feet!" And he leaped and walked. ¹¹Now when the people saw what Paul had done, they raised their voices, saying in the Lycaonian *language*, "The gods have come down to us in the likeness of men!"

Acts 16:16-18 ¹⁶Now it happened, as we went to prayer, that a certain slave girl possessed with a spirit of divination met us, who brought her masters much profit by fortune-telling. ¹⁷This girl followed Paul and us, and cried out, saying, "These men are the servants of the Most High God, who proclaim to us the way of salvation." ¹⁸And this she did for many days. But Paul, greatly annoyed, turned and said to the spirit [demon], "I command you in the name of Jesus Christ to come

out of her. And he came out that very hour."
(See Mark 16:17)

Acts 19:11-12 [11]Now God worked unusual miracles by the hands of Paul, [12]so that even handkerchiefs or aprons were brought from his body to the sick, and the diseases left them and the evil spirits went out of them.
(See Mark 16:16-17)

Acts 20:9-10 [9]And in a window sat a certain young man named Eutychus, who was sinking into a deep sleep. He was overcome by sleep; and as Paul continued speaking, he fell down from the third story and was taken up dead. [10]But Paul went down, fell on him, and embracing *him* said, "Do not trouble yourselves, for his life is in him."

14

Why Consider Paul?

With all Paul's offences against the Christians, why would the Lord Jesus have even considered choosing Paul to be the twelfth apostle? Was it possibly because of Paul's mindset and unstoppable desire to be the very best in whatever he did to please his masters—whether it be outstanding good or bad? Could it be that the Savior saw in Paul an energetic, tireless, zealous, high achiever who had confessed, repented, and absolutely turned completely toward God to literally devote his life to serve? And, still, in humility, Paul writes:

> **1 Corinthians 15:9** For I am the least of the apostles and do not even deserve to be called an apostle, because I persecuted the church of God. (NIV)

We can respect and appreciate Paul's humbleness, but at the same time we can see that he was bold and courageous. He stood up to Peter the apostle and pointed out that Peter was being hypocritical:

Galatians 2:9-16 ⁹and when James, Cephas, and John, who seemed to be pillars, perceived the grace that had been given to me [to lead Gentiles to Christ], they gave me and Barnabas the right hand of fellowship, that we should go to the Gentiles and they to the circumcised. (Acts 10:28) ¹⁰*They desired* only that we should remember the poor, the very thing which I also was eager to do. (Acts 11:29-30) ¹¹Now when Peter had come to Antioch, I withstood him to his face, because he was to be blamed, ¹²for before certain men came from James, he would eat with the Gentiles, but when they came, he withdrew himself, fearing those who were of the circumcision. ¹³And the rest of the Jews also played the hypocrite with him, so that even Barnabas was carried away with their hypocrisy. ¹⁴But when I saw that they were not straightforward about the truth of the gospel, I said to Peter before *them all*, "If you, being a Jew, live in the manner of the Gentiles and not as the Jews, why do you compel Gentiles to live as Jews?" ¹⁵"We *who are* Jews by nature, and not sinners of the Gentiles," ¹⁶"knowing that a man is not justified [to be saved for eternal life in heaven] by the works of the law but by faith in Jesus Christ, even we have believed in Christ Jesus, that we might be justified by faith in Christ and not by works of the law; for by the works of the law no flesh shall be justified."

Galatians 2:19-21 ¹⁹"For if I through the law died to the law that I might live to God." ²⁰"I have been crucified with Christ; it is no longer I who live, but Christ lives in me; and the *life* which I now live in the flesh I live by faith in the Son of God, who loved me and gave Himself for me." [21]"I do not set aside the grace of God, for if righteousness comes through the law, then Christ died in vain," [If we could save ourselves, then the Lord Jesus Christ died for nothing.]

But Paul also, near the end of his life, sufferings, and service, wrote:

1 Timothy 1:12-17 [12]I thank Christ Jesus our Lord, who has given me strength, that he considered me faithful, appointing me to his service. [13]even though I was once a blasphemer and a persecutor and a violent man, I was shown mercy because I acted in ignorance and unbelief. [14]The grace of our Lord was poured out on me abundantly, along with the faith and love that are in Christ Jesus. [15]Here is a trustworthy saying that deserves full acceptance: Christ Jesus came into the world to save sinners-of whom I am the worst. [16]But for that very reason I was shown mercy so that in me, the worst of sinners, Jesus Christ might display his unlimited patience as an example for those who would believe on him and receive eternal life. [17]Now to the King eternal, immortal, invisible, the only God, be honor and glory for ever and ever. Amen. (NIV)

15

How Can We Know?

How can we know whose name will be the Twelfth Name on the Wall Foundation?

2 Corinthians 12:12 Truly the signs of an apostle were accomplished among you with all perseverance, in signs and wonders and mighty deeds.

Paul always opened his Letters with a salutation identifying himself to the recipients.

Paul's introductory first verses tell us that he is an apostle of Jesus Christ by the will of God. In total, nine of his thirteen Epistles, eight of which are recorded below, state that he was a chosen apostle of Jesus Christ. The ninth such greeting will also be named; read on:

Romans 1:1 PAUL, a bondservant of Jesus Christ, called to be an apostle, separated to the gospel of God.

1 Corinthians 1:1 PAUL, called to be an apostle of Jesus Christ through the will of God, and Sosthenes our brother,

2 Corinthians 1:1a PAUL, an apostle of Jesus Christ by the will of God, and Timothy our brother,

(Galatians 1:1 is set aside until last.)

Ephesians 1:1a PAUL, an apostle of Jesus Christ by the will of God,
Colossians 1:1 PAUL, an apostle of Jesus Christ by the will of God, and Timothy our brother,
1 Timothy 1:1 PAUL, an apostle of Jesus Christ, by the commandment of God our Savior and the Lord Jesus Christ, our hope,
2 Timothy 1:1 PAUL, an apostle of Jesus Christ by the will of God, according to the promise of life which is in Christ Jesus.
Titus 1:1-3 PAUL, a bondservant of God and an apostle of Jesus Christ, according to the faith of God's elect and the acknowledgment of the truth which accords with godliness, ²in hope of eternal life which God, who cannot lie, promised before time began, ³but has in due time manifested His word through preaching, which was committed to me according to the commandment of God our Savior.

The only reason Paul did not begin each and every Letter the same way was because some of the letters were co-authored or co-written by brothers who were not chosen apostles. Since the Twelve were Personally chosen by the Lord Jesus Christ and by the will of God, Paul most likely did not

want to cause any confusion that the ones like Timothy and Silvanus might be among the Twelve. Therefore, it was best he left out the title on these four Epistles:
> **Philippians 1:1a** PAUL, and Timothy, bondservants of Jesus Christ.
> **1 Thessalonians 1:1a** PAUL, Silvanus, and Timothy,
> **2 Thessalonians 1:1a** PAUL, Silvanus, and Timothy,
> **Philemon 1:1a** PAUL, a prisoner of Christ Jesus, and Timothy our brother,

Returning now to the beginning: Consider two key points from Acts 1:23-24:
> **Acts 1:23b** *they... proposed two*
> **Acts 1:24b** *show which of these two You have chosen*

Paul's opening in the Letter to the Galatians seems to take on the assumption that Mathias was chosen by the *men* who were trying to tell God how *they* could begin the choosing for Him:
> **Galatians 1:1** PAUL, an apostle (not from men nor through man, but through Jesus Christ and God the Father who raised Him from the dead),

From the beginning of the chosen disciples, the Lord Jesus Personally chose each and every one to be God's future chosen Apostles. Notably, no other person named in the Bible, is claimed to be appointed to be an apostle by Jesus Christ.

However, the twelfth name is not a make it or break it matter. Each believer has freedom to believe what he will.

If we don't know, we should not be dogmatic. We will find out when we get up there!

> **Romans 14:5** One person considers one day more sacred than another; another man considers every day alike. Each one should be fully convinced in his own mind. (NIV)

Paul reminds us in three of his Epistles that arguing is not profitable:

> **1 Timothy 6:3-5** ³If anyone teaches otherwise and does not consent to wholesome words, *even* the words of our Lord Jesus Christ, and to the doctrine which accords with godliness, ⁴he is proud, knowing nothing, but is obsessed with disputes and arguments over words, from which come envy, strife, reviling, evil suspicions, ⁵useless wranglings of men of corrupt minds and destitute of the truth, who suppose that godliness is a *means of* gain. From such withdraw yourself.
>
> **2 Timothy 2:23** But avoid foolish and ignorant disputes, knowing that they generate strife.

Arguments become competitions to see who will win—when more often than not, there is no end to the dispute; the result is only discord, tension and hostility.

> **Titus 3:9** But avoid foolish controversies and genealogies and arguments and quarrels about the law, because these are unprofitable and useless. (NIV)

The intention of this book is not to promote, win or lose any arguments. The purpose is to give glory to God for the wonderful, miraculous strength with which he poured grace on Paul to lead so many souls to our Savior and God, the Lord Jesus Christ. The fruits of Paul's works are as effective today as they were when, in person, he was boldly and courageously spreading the Gospel message. He pleads with us:

> **1 Corinthians 1:10** I appeal to you, brothers, in the name of our Lord Jesus Christ, that all of you agree with one another so that there may be no divisions among you and that you may be perfectly united in mind and thought. (NIV)

When we all get there to see for ourselves, we will know who the twelfth apostle is.

Whose name will be
The Twelfth Name on the Wall Foundation?

A Note to the Reader

Thank you for reading our story. If you enjoyed *"The Twelfth Name on New Jerusalem's Wall Foundation"*, please consider leaving a written review on Amazon, Goodreads, Barnes & Noble, or wherever you found our book.

Reader reviews set the stage and are essential for the success of the book, especially for independently published authors like us.

Word-of-mouth ensures continued success. When a book has the potential to change lives, success for the book equals more lives changed.

We pray that *"The Twelfth Name on New Jerusalem's Wall Foundation"* will have an impact for the Lord, and maybe reach a soul for Him.

Connect with the Author
Please feel free to reach out to us with any questions.
You can reach Michael via

Website: https://michaelcopple.com

Email: mike@michaelcopple.com

Other Books by Michael

DIGGING DEEPER INTO THE REVELATION OF JESUS CHRIST – A STUDY GUIDE
Paperback ISBN 978-1-7389735-7-6
eBook ISBN 978-1-7389735-8-3

VASTNESS OF PACE – the color edition – Fiction
Paperback ISBN 978-1-777 8325-9-9
eBook ISBN 978-1-738 9735-0-7

VASTNESS OF PACE – the black/white edition
Paperback ISBN 978-1-738 9735-2-1
eBook ISBN 978-1-738 9735-3-8

SOLVING THE SPIRITUAL DILEMMA
Non-Fiction
Paperback ISBN 978-1-7778325-2-0
eBook ISBN 978-1-7778325-3-7

CONSIDERING WISDOM –Non-Fiction
Paperback ISBN 978-1-9736-9622-3
Hardcover ISBN 978-1-9736-9623-0
eBook ISBN 978-1-9736-9621-6

CALLING FROM THE SKY
A Novel inspired by True Events
Paperback ISBN 978-1-7778325-7-5
eBook ISBN 978-1-7778325-8-2

About the Author

Michael Copple's life experience includes twenty-six years active duty in the US Air Force, nine years of which were overseas, including one year in Vietnam, and nine years with the Wings of Blue Parachute Team at the U.S. Air Force Academy. From 1983 to 1986, he was the Superintendent of Parachuting Operations at USAF Academy. He has logged over 2,000 parachute jumps with fifteen hours of freefall, and earned jump wings from six foreign countries. Michael obtained the highest enlisted rank of Chief Master Sergeant.

He survived several near-death events including four parachute malfunctions, a night equipment jump entanglement with another jumper, being hung up to the outside of an aircraft at 3,000 feet above ground level, and he was caught in an 85mph wind shear under canopy—and more. You can read all about his parachute malfunctions and what it feels like in his novel "*Calling from the Sky*".

Michael realized that his God-given purpose is to devote his time to the Lord by bringing forth God's Word, moderating Bible studies, and authoring Christian literature, both Fiction and Non-Fiction. This has now been his goal since 2005.

Michael Copple has resided near Golden, B.C., with his Canadian wife, Elfriede, since 2003. They both believe that the Lord Jesus Christ is indeed the Son of God, enjoy reading and studying God's Word, cross country skiing, hiking, and walking every day with their dog.

Visit Michael and read more about him on his website/blog at: https://michaelcopple.com/

www.ingramcontent.com/pod-product-compliance
Lightning Source LLC
Chambersburg PA
CBHW071255070526
44583CB00017B/2477